Camera Obscura

Poems of Sight and Insight

Melinda B Hipple

First publication credits:

"Focus" - *Pirene's Fountain*, Sept. 2017;
"Camera Body," "Silver Anniversary," "Portrait Sitting," "Beetle,"
and "Coming Home" - *Watershed*, 2016;
"Monarch" - *Watershed*, 2014;
"Guernica," "Cataracts" - *Pirene's Fountain*, Nov. 2014;
"Equilibrium" - *Watershed*, 2013

Paperback ISBN 978-1-64254-028-4
Copyright ©Melinda B Hipple, 2018
Second Edition Paperback ISBN 978-1-64318-104-2
Copyright ©Melinda B Hipple, 2021

All rights reserved. No part of this publication may be reproduced, distributed, or transmitted in any form or by any means, including photocopying, recording, or other electronic or mechanical methods, without the prior written permission of the copyright holder, except in the case of brief quotations embodied in critical reviews and certain other noncommercial uses permitted by copyright law. For permission requests, write to the publisher, addressed "Attention: Permissions Coordinator," at the address below.

703 Eighth Street
Baldwin City, KS, 66006
www.imperiumpublishing.com

Camera Obscura

A number of these poems were presented at the 2016 Sigma Tau Delta (honorary English society) convention in Minneapolis, Minnesota.
Special thanks to Marti Mihalyi for her guidance in paring many of them down to their essence.

Contents

———————————————o◊o———————————————

4	The I in Eye	32	Earthquake
5	Slide Show	33	Equilibrium
6	Scars	34	Camera Body
7	Photographing My Mother-in-law	36	Fiction
8	Her *Other* Passion	37	The House Cook
9	Portrait Sitting	38	Coming Home
10	The Journalist and the Telepath	40	Silver Anniversary
11	Cataracts	41	Swarm
12	Monarch	42	Pigeon
13	Running Late	43	Diving Lesson
14	Beetle	44	Pendulum
15	A Pair	45	Paternal Grandmother
16	It Rained	46	The Psychiatrist
18	Focus	47	Fortunes of Childhood
19	Hello, It's Me	48	Summer Brother
22	Sweet Light	50	Play Things
23	Chimera	51	Postcard from Childhood
24	Disconnect	52	The Iris Garden
25	Dust	54	Inherited Things
26	Reading Hands	55	At My Mother's Passing
28	Guernica	56	Dust to Dust
30	The Calculation, 1925	57	She Sent Me Grandpa's Teeth
31	To Her Listening Ear	58	Sorting the Garage
	Responsive Chords of Music Came	60	Genetic Material

The I in Eye

It began with the axiom *write what you know*.
For years, I'd been *writing* with silver salts
on celluloid film, capturing light in a box.

After my father died, I focused (literally)
on my childhood—the most intimate subject
I could conjure. Perhaps a model, a young girl,
would play my part. If she could take direction,
we might uncover something worthwhile.

While sorting my father's things, I found my model
among the family slides. I spotted her by her eyes.
Blue-gray. Sullen. Often brimming with tears.
She would not need direction. I knew full well
she had already played my part.

slide show
_____o◊o_____

I strip naked in the studio, stand
in front of a projected series of poems
written to my dead father. A beam of light
tattoos angry words across my back,
speaks what I never could
while he was alive. I shift my body—
the canvas—and prepare
for the next slide.

I dress, turn to hug the final image—
me at the age of three,
larger than life, dressed
in urine-soaked overalls. The flash
from my father's camera glints
off of the pooled tears
that have waited forty years
to wet my cheeks.

Scars

He strips to his briefs and sits comfortably on a chair
while I photograph his thigh. The entry wound is small,
but when he twists to the back, the scar
quadruples in size. He recounts the incident—black jungle,
tracer fire, the metallic taste of fear. There was quick pain,
he explains. But nothing like the slow pain of healing.

I snap photos of his back, of the damage done
by a black widow who took offense when he
invaded her space. Click shots of the foot he barely felt
as a shard of glass hidden beneath water sliced through
from bottom to top.

Still naked, he begins to talk of his mother—
the days his father would drive him and his sisters
to the asylum for picnics on the lawn. He remembers
her bright red fingernails as she dug them into his arm.
The sudden, quick pain.

And the slow pain of healing.

Photographing My Mother-in-law

Don't retouch this she says, pointedly,
as if she knows I'm here to document
the painful past etched vividly into the folds
of her face.

Rumor has it there was a time
when only one person
occupied her head. She knows I know.
She lets me in.

Five frames later, her chin drops.

Enough.

The shutter snaps closed.

Her Other Passion

When she agreed to sit for me—
this hospice nurse with a soft Texas drawl—
I imagined the camera would capture
some glimpse of her gentile manner,
her compassion. Perhaps the sadness
that must accumulate
in her bones.

I did not imagine that she would slide
a pistol from her purse, break it down
and reassemble it in ten seconds flat, all the while
flashing a hint of the reassuring smile
she reserves for dying patients
and unsuspecting photographers.

Portrait Sitting

She pulls clothes, plastic flowers,
a sock monkey out of her bag,
sets them aside in the studio.
I click off a few shots. Turning
to the camera, she holds
a comb to her hair. A notepad
to her chest.
                "This represents
my first achievement and
my last achievement. I learned
to part my hair when I was four,
and this is the suicide note I wrote
yesterday."
                Stunned,
I lower the camera, but she pleads,
"Keep shooting. Just
keep shooting."

The Journalist and the Telepath

I am here for moral support
and maybe to protect her
from the evil eye. She talks.
Asks questions. I study the man
on the other side of the desk—
this "professor" of mind over matter.
Overweight. Half-shaven.
Slovenly. He speaks of voices
swimming in his head, techniques
for remembering backwards
into our past lives. The power
of a pyramid.

My friend makes her final notes
on paper. I make a few in my head.
No poison Kool-Aid here. Just
a hundred souls seeking answers
and one man hoping
for a free ride.

Cataracts

The fog is gone
from eyes surgically new.
Without time to adjust, to
grow into awareness,
she becomes the child
born wholly sentient, dropped
into a new world of dazzling hues,
crisp edges, a granddaughter's beauty
fully revealed. She has no time to adapt
to the age of her own skin in the mirror
even while the blue of her eyes
seems bluer looking in.

Monarch

She hangs weary at the browning edge
of the echinacea garden, her proboscis
curled in place, too tired to eat.
She has been battered by wind, scarred
by one narrow escape after another.
My hands—scarred and darkening—
steady the lens, pause
as I look for her best side.
She has no *best* side.
Glamour shots become documentary.
I wonder how old I would be
in butterfly years.

Running Late

He died with his wings folded forward—
the black-veined rust-colored chitin
pressed tightly against his fragile thorax,
his delicate abdomen. Perhaps
he thought it would save him. Perhaps
he only thought of Michhuahcān,
of Sierra Madre del Sur, of escaping
to a place he had never seen. If only
he could survive the night, the early frost.
Revive in the mid-morning sun. Exhaust himself
to reach the pine-oak forests where his ancestors
wintered beside the Purépecha, the Otomi.
The Nahua people.
                        His dream, his drive,
died on the pavement. His wings folded forward.
Hopeful.

Beetle

He's been dead for weeks now,
clinging to the window sheer as if
it was a natural place to expire.
I could pick him off. Toss him.
Flush him. I could flick him
loose and let him fall
to the floor behind the table.
Leave him as a curiosity
for the spider living there.

Old age. Starvation. Something
took him. Left him hanging
in his own little casket. Something
will take me one day as I lie
clinging to the sheer fabric
of life. Aging, starving,
I'll crawl up the side of a wall
and just stop living. Gawk
if you want to. But don't be sorry.
I've lived a very full beetle life.

A Pair

of zebra swallowtails
drift, then gently wing,
as if a small eddy of air
has taken on color,
and one brush of my hand
or one errant breeze
might dissolve the illusion

diaphanous wings
glow in a shaft of sun,
diminish in the shadows

they float, lift
above the green clipped lawn,
circle, flirt,
mate

and teach me to believe
in fairies

It Rained

———————————o◇o———————————

It began as mist dampening bone-crisp leaves
that ached beneath our mindless steps.
It swirled as fairy dust beneath umbrellas
and overhangs, tickled summer skin
into an autumn blush. Hurried into rivulets.
Ran the curbs. Filled small depressions
to be straddled, or not.

It grew to light rain. Soaked bare trees
to black. Spilled raindrop curtains from awnings
as shoppers at each entrance wondered
walk or run? It slapped the pavement
with syncopated rhythm, shifted beats
with each wind gust, tapped a relentless drip
that sent many a store clerk in search
of relief.

In late afternoon, one thunderclap
announced a downpour which set in for the day
and on into night. Fire bans would lift.
Grasses would feign one last greening
before winter. Folks from all walks
would sigh their relief. This relentless summer—
baked yellow-ocher into the landscape—
could now be put to memory.

Focus

Some days, I want to unpack
myself. Unbutton my skin, drape it
over the back of a chair. No longer worry
about wrinkles. Stack my bones
in the corner, and set aside this packet
of organs that keep a body humming.
I want to step out of the vulnerability.
Move through the world without
distraction. Discover a universal truth
not dependent on need
or tempted by want
or driven by fear.

Hello, It's Me (Just a little piece of fluff)

If I let loose this puff
this silky seed of milkweed pod
high into the air
into this blustery day,
would it travel—
skating the skies of October,
rounding the bend of November winds
to escape out to sea
before December's winter
frosted it to the ground?

Would it sail the air currents salted and swift,
buffet in April storm clouds
adrift over oceans of shadow,
skipping past schools of mackerel
and the lone whale's shape
or masses of glowing plankton
just breaking the surface?

Would it ride the updrafts,
roller-coastering its way across
continents of light, skimming the tips
of Kilimanjaro, Everest and Denali
on its way to Aconcagua
before dipping deep into the valley of death
or the great rift that slices worlds apart?

If I let loose this tiny thing
and it circled the globe
and circled again
because it wanted to take in the whole,
the everything of the earth,
the all of its beauty not nitpicked
down to the bone of what was ugly
in the microscopic lives
of non-milkweed existence,

if I did,
and sometime next October
it landed soft at your feet,
and you would pick it up,
holding it to the light,
watching its tiny strands of filament fingers
waving little hellos in the breeze,
would you know
it came from me?

Sweet Light

when Venus comes burning white
into a cobalt sky

when halogen vapor floods gold
onto the street

when the wind holds its breath
before exhaling a storm

that hour

before the stars can muster
their first silver dust

before we lie down in the dark
to hide our sins from the moon

Chimera

Through the glass
a fragile image wavers
pale behind reflected skies –

mirrored moments
overlapping in a quirk of time.

A sea away
your hair falls back
revealing ice behind your eyes.

My hands reach out
to shatter glass
and break, instead,
the charm of this illusion.

Disconnect

Moonbeams crawl across the floor
on the foot of a snail. A river
of pale sheets connect us in chaos,
but only in a moment
of regret. I will not reach for you
under this flower moon. I will
hold my breath and wait
a thousand years for you to smile.
And wait a thousand more.

Dust

        from a car long over the hill
eddies across the pasture turned
umber in the setting sun.
In a temporary fog, I replay
our first lovesick summer
in the fields.

Dust
      settles a stifling layer
over brittle prairie grass and stirs up
dry, crackling cicada song.
I turn back to the road
and remember why it is
I am making this trip
alone.

Reading Hands

I sculpted my hand in clay
and glazed it black—
my penchant for the morose.

I wonder how telling the read
if you could hold
this cold and lifeless bauble,
trace no lines across its palm
or find no fingerprint to explain
the who and why of me.

What would it say,
this objet d'art
pressing down a stack of books
to hold the history of art in place
as though Michelangelo, Miró and Mondrian
would flee the table top
without my pompous presence?

How would it speak
to my choices
that I preserve a piece of me
fired to the color of gunmetal
and fashioned
as if it were eternally reaching?

Tell me, if you can,
how to read this hand.

Guernica

_____o◊o_____
                              Oil on canvas by Pablo Picasso 1937

In this dance macabre,
a bull, a horse
close the distance
from horn to heart,
spill gray hope
upon Basque soil.

A beautiful brushstroke
no longer shakes us
from the glorified gore
of broken blades
and severed limbs.

These dagger tongues scream
of shifting dimensions,
of space out of time,

of a dark aftermath
where we will ride the chaos
on our knees.

And we will ride without surrender
for as long as Man finds honor
in the death of children.

The Calculation, 1925

———————————————o◇o———————————————
Oil on canvas by Joan Miró

Three minus four, a negative sum,
is quite the abstraction for one so young.

      Hungry for his art
      as much as for food,
      he lets deprivation
      open a portal
      to the subconscious.
      Automatism reigns.

When we reckon the sum of three minus four,
a negative number is what's in store.

      The surrealists' tool
      exposes a psychic guide
      manipulating brush strokes
      and meticulous detail
      without censure. He tells us
      only children *play* at art.

A negative four plus a positive three
scrambles the brains of the relative we.

To Her Listening Ear Responsive Chords of Music Came
_____o◇o_____
19th Century oil by Edwin Longsden Long

She dismisses us for just a moment—
this young woman whose captivating gaze
would otherwise meet our own.

With the lute pushed aside,
with the turn of her head,
her longing becomes ours. We turn
to spy her companion, her lover,
some distant mystery set to music.

She dismisses us. And, for a moment,
we dismiss the boundaries
of canvas
              and frame
                        and time.

Earthquake

_____o◇o_____

Her body shimmers with silver coins
scattered about the layers of delicate fabric
gathered at her hips. "It starts in the feet,"
she explains barefoot in front of the class.
After hours of instruction in *danse oriental*,
we are both spent and energized. "Concentrate
on your feet. Feel the earth begin to tremble.
Feel the vibration climb from your heels
to your ankles. Your knees. Your hips."

We feel nothing, at first. Then the fast-twitch
muscle fibers in our calves and thighs
fire neurons from fatigue, begin to quiver.
We heed our bodies. Find our rhythm.
And slowly, a room full of coins
begins to sing.

Equilibrium

In equal amounts,
a rainbow of color muddies
to a safe and neutral gray.
Passionate red gives up its angst.
Blue surfaces from the depths
of depression. Yellow hides
its zealous cheer behind dull eyes.

Gray, the lithium of color, reins in
the mayhem. Stabilizes extremes.

In a madhouse of color, gray
is the man in the white coat
holding the little black bag.

Camera Body

Even without a camera in my hands
I walk with a photographer's eye, notice
some piece of chaff that flutters
against the wind—
                            butterfly

a flake of leaf not quite the right
shade of green—
                            katydid

constant motion in the nettles
on a still day—
                            bees

I also walk to listen with
a photographer's ear, to hear
the quiet chuck of a mother robin
at attention—
                            fledgling

a steady whee rippling the air at
the water's surface—
spring peeper

the unfamiliar chirp of a sparrow
in pain—
broken wing

And when a novice says *you must have
a really good camera*, I glance
at my empty hands and say, *yes,
yes, I do.*

Fiction

Sometimes I make stuff up—
pretend a being into being,
give it a face, a name,
something to overcome.
I fabricate a life on paper.

But the character is shallow,
so I flay a piece of my flesh
and scribe it to the page.

The House Cook

Her place was in the kitchen,
knees tucked under the same counter
where she seasoned cuts of beef,
flattened pie crust. Ate her meals.
She sat opposite us, isolated
on the stool next to the stove.
She handed out burgers, corn, leftovers,
retrieved milk from the fridge.
From our vantage point next to Dad
at the raised bar, we looked down
on her position. Ate staring into her face—
a face that avoided my father's gaze,
winced almost imperceptibly
at the sound of his voice.
When she thought no one was home,
she stood at the sink, cried,
argued with the air to get
                        the last word.

Coming Home

I used to work here, she said.
During the war. It was
a Pratt and Whitney plant then.

Thanks to my under bite,
we spent every Saturday
for two years driving into the city
of her past. Once there,
we made a day of it. Lunch.
A museum. The opera. She would
wait out my appointment—
five minutes to tighten my braces—
then drive us past
the downtown library.

I used to work here,
she told me. *After the war.*
I got the job because I told them
how much I loved to read.

Sometimes we simply cruised
the neighborhoods—Waldo,
Brookside, Ward Parkway
Estates—just to check out
the architecture. She'd slow,
pull to the curb. Point.

*I like the way they built that
overhang. See how the gable
cuts down over the door to
block the rain.*

When there were no more excuses,
she'd drive us out of the city—
the glitter in her eyes fading
to rural darkness—toward home.

Silver Anniversary

Whole, the swan was pretty
in a dime-store kitsch sort of way.
Oh, but it was beautiful
when it caught fire—
pink netting succumbing
to the chemistry of anger,
flaming down to its wire bones.

Swarm

He stood an even six foot. Handsome,
except for his polyester jumpsuits
and goofy grin. He was mean-spirited,
busy. Raised cows, chickens, horses,
pigeons, guppies. He let his wife
raise the children.

Bees. He raised bees in a yard
where children played tag and statue
and mother-may-I. Or, would have,
if it hadn't been for the bees.
When they swarmed, he drove his pickup
through the yard, built and climbed
a scaffold tower, hoisted a wooden box
into the treetops, picked off bees one by one
until he found the queen. Barehanded,
he coaxed her into a new house,
and her following   followed.

When his children got too close,
he let his wife tend the stings.

Pigeon

You poked the eye dropper
into his gaping beak, squeezed mash
into the squab's belly. His morning ration.
You held him in the cage of your fingers,
trapped, but not too tightly. I saw the blue bulges,
skin-covered eyes that strained to see
this awkward man-mother that fed him daily.
I marveled at how gentle you could be
with someone else's child.

Diving Lesson

Here—eighteen feet above the river,
hand on my nose, eyes closed,
milliseconds after the leap—
I'm suspended on film.
I still expect to feel a sting
as the soles of my feet slap water,
that restrained panic in my lungs
as I struggle to the surface
for air.

You shamed me into the risk.
Yet, I learned I could survive
even you.

Pendulum

_____o◇o_____

You saw in me what provoked
your own childhood demons,
and so you stabbed at it,
changed to its polar opposite
that which I now carve
at the heart of my child
in desperation
to change back again.

Paternal Grandmother

She knitted sweaters I could not wear.
Hand feather-stitched a Sixties psychedelic
polyester double-knit crazy quilt that would not
die. Misspelled my name on birthday cards
because she knew my parents had got it
wrong. Refused to walk fifty yards
for one of my recitals that were held in the
wrong church. Counted the years I was married
without children. Spent decades trying to be
the grandparent she thought I needed.

The Psychiatrist

Everyone else had left the table. Siblings
ran off to play. Grandma tended to the cleanup.
My parents walked off their dispute, though
never to a resolution. Grandpa and I—
who preferred our meat well done—gnawed
at our leather steaks.

Gruff, whiskered, the gray of his hair
leaching into his skin, Grandpa straightened
on the bench. "Ya know, hon," he said,
clearing his throat. "Your parents' problems.
They ain't your fault."

I nodded and went back to chewing
a little easier this time.

Fortunes of Childhood

Grandpa standing by the fire
to poke at something important,
his pipe smoke layered
just above my reach.
The mantel clock's thin
metal strike muffled
in Grandma's chest, lost
in the booming rumble of her words
as the vibration and the warmth
carry me to sleep.

Summer Brother

―――――――――――――o◇o―――――――――――――

The mud was warm and free of leeches this day—
our feet sucking in and out along the banks,
our eyes searching for the thing that would be revealed
and give us reason to continue.

"Watch for snakes," you warned just to see me
dart my eyes the length of the bend
and back to your impish smile, oh dear brother.
We saddled a log and moved on.

"Have you ever eaten one of these?" you asked,
small red berries extended on your palm.
I trusted you not to poison me but turned them down.
I wouldn't eat what cows refused.

Grabbing a stick, you nudged a stack of silted leaves
just under the surface, and the fattest pollywog
slithered away—its hind legs not yet broken out.
The current churned the mud downstream.

With gray Missouri clay caked just below my knees,
I followed you the length of the creek.
You showed me where to spy the crawdad's hole
and how to send him backwards, fingers still intact.

And once, when I'd snagged my shorts in gooseberry
briars and couldn't untangle my way to freedom,
you spared a minute for my struggle, even helped
to pick the sticktights from my shirt.

You and I seldom fought in private. We needed
audience for that, and so we walked the stream,
dared to hold each other's hands across
the fallen obstacles, the wooden tightropes.

While we squandered hours in the sticky heat of August,
we never told each other how we felt about
being born as kin, but I appreciate it more as I look
backward into the filtered light of childhood.

Play Things

Chatty Cathy—her hair plugs visible
from one too many haircuts, one eye
missing, a voice like gravel
when you pull the string

A box of buckeyes, broken arrowheads,
mussel shells from the riverbank

Barbie—one foot mangled by the
chihuahua—covered in pin holes
and scuff marks from G. I. Joe's
strategic attacks

Snakes, snails, toads
that never lived long, cats
that never stayed long

A horse with the patience of a saint

Postcard from Childhood

It was the winter of
twelve inches—a perfect
porcelain white foot
of snow. Igloos
in Missouri. Galoshes
with too many socks.
Pond ice, creek ice.
Rapid streams fringed
in glass. Rabbit tracks,
bird tracks, fox trails.
A white horse lost
in a white woods.

The Iris Garden

I sat with feet folded back,
the soles of my white sandals pressed
into the bottom of my seersucker shorts.
The cool winter-soaked earth—still moist
from the last April snow—drew the new
spring warmth out of my dimpled shins.
The dirt was play, but not to my father.

I tended my marigold patch, plucked
stray grass, watched ants navigate
the rough terrain. My marigolds
were still looking for their courage.
"How long?" I asked. "A week," he said.
The wait was intolerable, but not for my father.

I turned to watch him work the rows,
pluck weeds, add mulch, cradle his iris bulbs
in heavy hands. I watched him prove
his gentle side, wished I could be
that iris bulb. I knew we were as close

as we would get. It was never enough, though
it seemed to be for my father.

Every year, spring promised a chance,
but every year I left the garden, jealous
of my marigolds. They offered their best.
I left it lie upon the May-flowered ground,
seeping back into the summer soil
to fertilize next year's hope.
I felt betrayed. But so did my father.

Our final spring together, he took me
to his garden. Pointing, naming,
plucking blooms, he thrust an iris in my hand.
I felt the petals rest remarkably light,
soft on my palm. And there it was—
his gentle side. I leaned in, cautiously,
to offer a hug.
                      And so did he.

Inherited Things

My father's paintings. The studied amateur.   *check*

Great Aunt Effie's chest of drawers
which he restored with contact paper.   *check*

World War II medals and photos of him
in uniform. I never knew he served.   *check*

A pigeon trophy. He was so busy with
his pigeons, flowers, guppies.   *check*

An antique side-by-side shotgun/rifle
and the story of his great-grandfather,
his grandmother and a murdered farmhand.   *check*

"Animals I Have Known." An essay
in his own hand with a B+ in the corner.
How sad he had to drown the little foxes.   *check*

The only thing of his that means anything
to me, personally—diabetes and the sense
of helplessness that accompanies it.   c*heck*

At My Mother's Passing

                                        Prose cutting from *The Secret Language of Art*,
                                        by Sarah Carr-Gomm, 2008

We placed her in the sky
   with the goddess of dawn
   caught in perpetual spring among
   gardens of countless flowers.

We placed her in the sky
   on horses whiter than snow
   as Zephyr blew from shores
   warmed by the sun god.

At last immortal and ageless,
   she embraced the moon, released
   the mountains, river and lakes,
   as we placed her in the sky.

Dust to Dust

I fashion mourning
from a box, paper, glue,
an old photo. Why not
a little glitter? Why not.
She would have smiled.

I craft my sorrow to
appeal to the eye. To
follow the aesthetic principles
of art. I make the grade.
I display it on a shelf.

For months, I do not touch it—
the box. The sorrow.

She Sent Me Grandpa's Teeth

in a box. Through the mail.
We'd found his dentures among the things
my mother hoarded. I'd forgotten
that I wanted them. Forgotten why.
Friends and I would gasp, then laugh
(at Mom's expense) each time
I opened the box to shock someone new.
Why on earth would she keep them?
Then again, why on earth
would I?

After the joke had been played out,
I looked for a suitable nook in which
to store the box.

Sorting the Garage

Peanut butter jars—clean,
neatly layered in boxes, waiting
to be filled or recycled.
A box of *National Geographics*
and the missing stock certificate.

A small wooden shelf holding
brittle, yellowed textbooks
from the one-room schoolhouse
she attended as a child.

Jars of rusted bolts, jars
of rusted washers, jars
of rusted screws.
A cardboard box stacked
with newspapers, spiders,
the missing silverware.

The eighty-year-old mattress
she had stuffed with down
that she had plucked by hand.

Lawn chairs, cove molding, nails
waiting to be straightened and reused.
A rusted tobacco tin containing
a plastic candy wrapper full of
gold dust.

And fifty years of letters
addressed from each
of her four children.

Genetic Material

Delicate strands of literary
DNA—a helix of words
twisting ink into meaning,
ideas into insight—
bond phrases, separate plot lines,
multiply meter, recombine
shifting heritable markers
down the paper matrix
from mother to daughter
as bookworm begets author.

www.ingramcontent.com/pod-product-compliance
Lightning Source LLC
Chambersburg PA
CBHW081158070526
44583CB00021B/2902